PUFFINS

AND

PENGUINS

BY ARNOLD RINGSTAD

The Child's World®
childsworld.com

Published by The Child's World®
1980 Lookout Drive • Mankato, MN 56003-1705
800-599-READ • www.childsworld.com

Photographs ©: Adam Sharp Photography/
Shutterstock Images, cover (puffin), 3, 11, 20, 24
(puffin); Kotomiti Okuma/Shutterstock Images,
cover (penguin), 2, 15, 21, 24 (penguin); Vlad
Silver/Shutterstock Images, 5, 13; Faheem Ahmed/
Shutterstock Images, 6; Lukas Fendek/Shutterstock
Images, 9; Rudmer Zwerver/Shuttestock Images, 10;
Robert McGillivray/Shutterstock Images, 14; Ondrej
Prosicky/Shutterstock Images, 17; Johnny Giese/
Shutterstock Images, 19

ISBN 9781503835962
LCCN 2019943065

Printed in the United States of America

ABOUT THE AUTHOR

Arnold Ringstad is the author
of more than 80 books for
kids. He lives in Minnesota
with his wife and their cat.

TABLE OF CONTENTS

Birds of the Coast

A bird dives into the sea. It uses its wings to swim. Sunlight flashes over its black and white feathers. The bird dives deeper. It grabs a fish in its mouth. Then it rises to the surface. Is it a puffin or a penguin? How are they different?

Penguins are black and white sea birds.

Puffins get their name from their puffy-looking bodies.

Puffins

Puffins are small birds. There are four kinds of puffins. The largest weigh less than 2 pounds (0.9 kg). They are 14 inches (0.36 m) tall. Puffins have black and white feathers. Most have white faces. The birds have big, brightly colored **beaks**.

Puffins live in the **Northern Hemisphere**. Many live in Iceland. Puffins build nests on sea cliffs. They dig **burrows** between rocks. This keeps them safe from **predators**.

Puffins' burrows sometimes have many tunnels.

Puffins can carry many fish in their beaks.

Puffins are great flyers. They can fly at 55 miles per hour (88 km/h). Puffins can swim, too. They dive into the water. They can stay underwater for about 30 seconds. Puffins have spikes in their mouths. This helps them grab fish. They can carry many fish at once!

Penguins

There are 17 kinds of penguins. The biggest ones weigh 90 pounds (40 kg). They stand almost 4 feet (1.2 m) tall. Penguins have white bellies. Their backs are black. Most also have black faces. Some have orange or yellow markings, too.

Emperor penguins are the largest type of penguin.

Penguins slide on their bellies to cross snow and ice. This is faster than walking.

Penguins live in the **Southern Hemisphere**. Some live in Antarctica. Others live in South America and Africa.

Penguins cannot fly. They are too heavy. However, their wings work great for swimming. The wings act like **flippers**. They let penguins zoom through the water. Penguins can swim at 20 miles per hour (32 km/h).

Penguins can dive deep into the sea. They can go down 1,850 feet (560 m). They can stay underwater for 20 minutes. They hunt fish in the sea.

Penguins can leap out of the water to escape predators.

What's the Difference?

Puffins and penguins have many differences. One difference is size. Puffins are much smaller. The biggest puffins are smaller than the smallest penguins.

Another difference is flight. Puffins are great fliers. Puffins can fly fast. Penguins are too heavy to fly.

Puffins are sometimes called "sea clowns" because of their brightly colored beaks.

But penguins are better swimmers.
Both puffins and penguins are amazing birds of the coast!

PUFFINS

- Live in the Northern Hemisphere
- Can stay underwater for about 30 seconds
- Can be as tall as 14 inches (0.36 m)

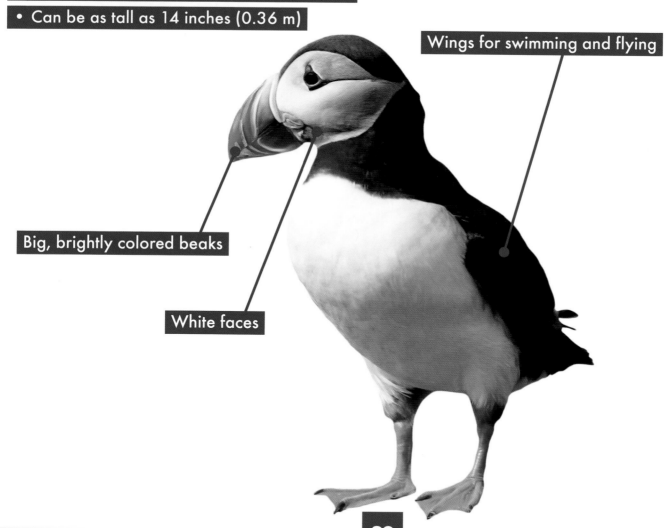

Wings for swimming and flying

Big, brightly colored beaks

White faces

PENGUINS

Yellow or orange markings

Black faces

Wings for swimming

- Live in the Southern Hemisphere
- Can stay underwater for about 20 minutes
- Can be as tall as 4 feet (1.2 m)

GLOSSARY

beaks (BEEKS) Beaks are the outside parts of a bird's mouth. Puffins use their beaks to grab fish.

burrows (BURR-ohs) Burrows are holes or tunnels made by animals for shelter. Puffins dig burrows between rocks on sea cliffs.

flippers (FLIP-erz) Flippers are flat parts of animals that help them swim. Penguin wings can act like flippers.

Northern Hemisphere (NOR-thurn HEM-ih-sfere) The Northern Hemisphere is the northern half of Earth. Puffins live in the Northern Hemisphere.

predators (PRED-uh-turs) Predators are animals that hunt and eat other animals. Puffins must watch out for predators.

Southern Hemisphere (SUTH-urn HEM-ih-sfere) The Southern Hemisphere is the southern half of Earth. Penguins live in the Southern Hemisphere.

TO LEARN MORE

IN THE LIBRARY

Beer, Julie. *Penguins vs. Puffins*. Washington, DC: National Geographic Kids, 2017.

Esbaum, Jill. *Penguins*. Washington, DC: National Geographic, 2014.

Reinke, Beth Bence. *The Frozen March of Emperor Penguins*. Mankato, MN: The Child's World, 2018.

ON THE WEB

Visit our website for links about puffins and penguins:
childsworld.com/links

Note to Parents, Teachers, and Librarians: We routinely verify our Web links to make sure they are safe and active sites. So encourage your readers to check them out!

ACTIVITY

Draw a picture of a puffin and a penguin. Your picture should clearly show the differences between the puffin and the penguin. Look at pages 20 and 21 for help.

INDEX